102

Kentucky

by Patricia K. Kummer
Capstone Press
Geography Department

Consultant:
Lisa Gross
Program Coordinator
Kentucky State Department of Education

CAPSTONE
HIGH/LOW BOOKS
an imprint of Capstone Press
Mankato, Minnesota

Capstone High/Low Books are published by Capstone Press
818 North Willow Street • Mankato, MN 56001
http://www.capstone-press.com

Library of Congress Cataloging-in-Publication Data
Kummer, Patricia K.
    Kentucky/by Patricia K. Kummer [and] Capstone Press Geography Department.
    p. cm. — (One nation)
    Includes bibliographical references and index.
    Summary: An overview of the state of Kentucky, including its history, geography,
people, and living conditions.
    ISBN 0-7368-0020-4
    1. Kentucky—Juvenile literature. [1. Kentucky.] I. Capstone Press. Geography
Dept. II. Title. III. Series.
F451.3.K86 1999
976.9—dc21
                                                          98-3161
                                                            CIP
                                                            AC

Editorial Credits
Timothy W. Larson, editor; Timothy Halldin, cover designer and illustrator;
    Sheri Gosewisch, photo researcher
Photo Credits
Churchill Downs, 6, 8
Craig W. Davis, cover, 34
David N. Davis, 26
Eddie Eller, 4 (bottom)
Jack Glisson, 10
James P. Rowan, 25
One Mile Up Inc., 4 (top)
Photophile/Mark E. Gibson, 16, 18; Jeff Greenberg, 21; Tom Tracy, 30
Unicorn Stock Photos/Chris Boylan, 5 (top); Martha McBride, 5 (bottom), 14, 38; Paul
    Murphy, 22; Mike Morris, 29; Jean Higgins, 33

Table of Contents

Fast Facts about Kentucky

State flag

Location: In the east-central United States

Size: 40,411 square miles (104,664 square kilometers)

Population: 3,908,124 (United States Census Bureau, 1997 estimate)

Capital: Frankfort

Date admitted to the Union: June 1, 1792; the 15th state

Kentucky cardinal

Goldenrod

Largest cities: Louisville, Lexington, Owensboro, Covington, Bowling Green, Hopkinsville, Paducah, Frankfort, Henderson, Ashland

Nickname: The Bluegrass State

State bird: Kentucky cardinal

State flower: Goldenrod

State tree: Kentucky coffee tree

State song: "My Old Kentucky Home" by Stephen Foster

Kentucky coffee tree

Chapter 1

The Kentucky Derby

The Kentucky Derby is one of the most famous horse races in the United States. It takes place every year on the first Saturday of May. Churchill Downs racetrack in Louisville hosts this race. More than 130,000 fans attend the derby each year. Millions of people around the world watch the derby on television.

Only thoroughbreds that are three years old run in the Kentucky Derby. A thoroughbred is a breed of horse born and raised for racing. Many of the derby's thoroughbreds are born on Kentucky horse farms.

The Kentucky Derby is one of the most famous horse races in the United States.

The Kentucky Derby's winning horse receives a blanket of red roses.

Kentucky Derby History

The Kentucky Derby is the nation's oldest annual horse race. The first Kentucky Derby occurred at Churchill Downs in 1875. Churchill Downs was called the Jockey Club then. The race has taken place at Churchill Downs every year since the first derby.

The Kentucky Derby's track was one and one-half miles (2.4 kilometers) long until 1896.

In that year, derby officials decided this distance was too tiring for the horses. The officials shortened the track to one and one-quarter miles (two kilometers). The track is still one and one-quarter miles long.

The horse Aristides won the first Kentucky Derby. He ran the race in two minutes and 37.75 seconds. Oliver Lewis was Aristides' jockey. A jockey is a person who rides horses in races.

In 1973, the horse Secretariat ran the fastest Kentucky Derby. Secretariat ran the race in one minute and 59.4 seconds. Secretariat is the only horse to run the derby in less than two minutes. Ron Turcotte was Secretariat's jockey.

Kentucky Derby Traditions

The Kentucky Derby has many traditions. A tradition is a practice continued over many years. For example, a band plays "My Old Kentucky Home" before each race starts. This song is Kentucky's state song.

The owner of the winning horse receives the Kentucky Derby Trophy and up to $700,000. The winning horse receives a blanket of red roses. People nicknamed the derby the Run for the Roses because of this tradition.

Chapter 2
The Land

Kentucky is in the east-central United States.
Seven other states are Kentucky's neighbors.
Indiana and Ohio border Kentucky to the north.
West Virginia and Virginia are Kentucky's
eastern neighbors. Tennessee lies to the south.
Missouri and Illinois lie to the west.

Kentucky has many kinds of land.
Mountains stand in eastern Kentucky. Grassy
hills roll across the middle of the state.
Swamps cover far southwestern Kentucky.
A swamp is an area of low, wet land.

The Appalachian Plateau

Eastern Kentucky is part of the Appalachian
Plateau. Thick forests cover much of the

Thick forests cover much of eastern Kentucky.

plateau. One-third of Kentucky's coal is in this area. The coal lies in pockets beneath the ground called deposits.

The Cumberland and Pine Mountains stand on the plateau. Black Mountain is one of the Cumberland Mountains. This peak is Kentucky's highest point. It rises 4,145 feet (1,263 meters) above sea level. Sea level is the average surface level of the world's oceans.

The Bluegrass Region

The Bluegrass region is in north-central Kentucky. Thick bluegrass covers fields in this

12

region. Bluegrass is green but sometimes looks blue in the morning sunlight. Kentuckians nicknamed their state the Bluegrass State after this grass.

Tobacco and corn crops grow well in the Bluegrass region. Many of Kentucky's largest cities also lie in this area.

The Pennyroyal Region

The Pennyroyal region covers south-central Kentucky. Pennyroyal is a plant with purple or blue flowers that grows throughout south-central Kentucky. Kentuckians named the Pennyroyal region after this plant.

Many caves lie underground in the Pennyroyal region. Mammoth Cave is one of these caves. It is the world's longest cave. It stretches nearly 400 miles (644 kilometers).

Western Kentucky

The Western Coal Field lies in northwestern Kentucky. Two-thirds of Kentucky's coal deposits lie underground there.

The Jackson Purchase region covers southwestern Kentucky. People named this area

Kentucky Lake is one of Kentucky's largest lakes.

after General Andrew Jackson. He purchased the region from the Chickasaw people in 1818.

Farmland covers most of the Jackson Purchase region. But swampy lowlands also lie in the area. Kentucky's lowest point is in the lowlands near Hickman. The land there is 257 feet (78 meters) above sea level.

Rivers and Lakes

Four rivers form most of Kentucky's borders. The Big Sandy and Tug Fork Rivers form

Kentucky's northeastern border. The Ohio River flows along Kentucky's northern and northwestern borders. The Mississippi River forms Kentucky's southwestern border

The Licking River, the Kentucky River, the Cumberland River, and the Tennessee River flow through Kentucky. All of these rivers empty into the Ohio River.

Kentucky's largest lakes include Kentucky Lake, Lake Barkley, and Lake Cumberland. These lakes formed when the U.S. government built dams on the Tennessee and Cumberland Rivers. Water backed up behind the dams and formed the lakes.

Climate

Kentucky has mild temperatures throughout the year. Average temperatures range from 22 to 86 degrees Fahrenheit (-6 to 30 degrees Celsius).

An average of 38 inches (97 centimeters) of rain falls in Kentucky each year. Southern Kentucky receives most of this rainfall. The state receives an average of 12 inches (30 centimeters) of snow each year. Most of this snow falls in the southeastern mountains.

Chapter 3

The People

Kentucky's city populations and rural populations are nearly equal. People in rural areas live away from large cities.

About 52 percent of Kentuckians live in cities. Three of the state's four largest cities are in the Bluegrass region. Louisville is the largest of these cities. Nearly 1 million people live in and around Louisville.

About 48 percent of Kentucky's population live in rural areas. Most of the state's rural population is scattered across the western and southern regions. Fewer people live in Kentucky's Appalachian Plateau region.

Louisville is one of the largest cities in Kentucky. Nearly 1 million people live in and around Louisville.

About 7 percent of Kentuckians are African Americans.

European Backgrounds

About 92 percent of Kentuckians have European backgrounds. Some of their families were among the state's first European settlers.

Kentucky's first European settlers arrived in the 1770s. They came from Pennsylvania, Virginia, and North Carolina. These early settlers had English, Scottish, and German backgrounds.

Most early settlers built large farms in the Bluegrass region. Others settled on small farms in the Appalachian Mountains.

In the 1800s, more settlers came to Kentucky directly from Europe. Many German people settled in Louisville and Covington. Many Irish people settled in eastern Kentucky.

African Americans

Most of the first African Americans to live in Kentucky were slaves. They worked on Kentucky's farms and tobacco plantations. Many of Kentucky's plantations grew tobacco as a main crop.

By 1860, nearly 211,000 African American slaves lived in Kentucky. But about 10,500 free African Americans also lived in the state. In 1865, Congress freed all African Americans in the nation. Congress is the elected body of the U.S. government that makes laws.

By the 1900s, Kentucky and other southern states had passed segregation laws. Kentucky's segregation laws kept African Americans and whites apart.

In the 1960s, many Kentuckians worked to change segregation laws in Kentucky. Now Kentucky has new laws that say all people should have equal rights.

Today, about 7 percent of Kentuckians are African Americans. Many of Kentucky's African Americans live and work in the state's cities.

Other Ethnic Groups

Less than 1 percent of Kentuckians have Asian, Hispanic, or Native American backgrounds. But Kentucky's Asian and Hispanic populations are growing.

Many Asian Americans in Kentucky have families that came to Kentucky from China, India, or the Philippines. Other families came to Kentucky from South Korea.

Most Hispanic Americans in Kentucky have families that came from Spanish-speaking countries. Many of these families came to Kentucky from Mexico or Puerto Rico.

Most Native Americans in Kentucky have Cherokee, Shawnee, or Creek backgrounds.

Most Native Americans living in Kentucky have Cherokee, Shawnee, or Creek backgrounds.

They live and work throughout the state. Some Native Americans still speak their native languages and live traditional lives. They practice the styles, manners, and ways of the past.

Chapter 4
Kentucky History

People have lived in the area that is now Kentucky for about 12,000 years. Native Americans were the first people to live there. The Mississippian people lived in the area about 1,000 years ago. They built large burial mounds along the Mississippi River.

By the 1700s, many Native American groups lived in the area that is now Kentucky. They built villages and grew crops there. These groups included the Cherokee, the Chickasaw, the Creek, and the Shawnee peoples.

The Mississippian people lived in what is now Kentucky about 1,000 years ago. Today, scientists study the bones of these people.

The Wilderness Trail and Settlement

In 1775, Daniel Boone led a group of 30 settlers into the area that is now Kentucky. The group entered the region near the Cumberland Gap. The gap provided an opening between the Cumberland Mountains through which the group could travel.

Boone's group widened a Native American trail from the Cumberland Gap to the Kentucky River. The group named this trail the Wilderness Trail. Boone's group built a settlement at the end of the Wilderness Trail near present-day Boonesboro. The settlement was one of the first European settlements in the area.

Revolutionary War

In April 1775, the American colonies went to war with Great Britain to gain their independence. This was the Revolutionary War (1775–1783). Boone and other settlers fought for the colonies. They protected settlements in the area that is now Kentucky.

On September 3, 1783, Great Britain officially surrendered and the Revolutionary War ended. The colonies won their

Daniel Boone and his group built a settlement at the end of the Wilderness Trail.

independence and became the United States of America.

Statehood

By 1790, nearly 74,000 settlers lived in the area that is now Kentucky. Many of these settlers wanted their own state. On June 1, 1792, Kentucky became the 15th U.S. state. Frankfort became its capital in 1793.

Some Kentuckians fought for the Confederate States of America during the Civil War.

Kentucky's population grew quickly. By 1840, the state had 779,828 people.

Horse farming also grew quickly. Kentucky's horse farmers raised more horses than farmers from other states did.

The Civil War

By 1860, slavery divided the nation. Slavery was illegal in Northern states. But it was legal in Southern states. People in Southern states feared the U.S. government would end slavery.

In 1861, 11 Southern states left the United States. These states formed a new country called the Confederate States of America. Kentucky stayed with the United States.

On April 12, 1861, the United States and the Confederate States of America went to war. This was the Civil War (1861–1865). Some Kentuckians fought for the United States. Others fought for the Confederate States of America.

In April 1865, the Confederate States of America surrendered. On December 6, 1865, Congress passed a law that made slavery illegal in all states.

Changes in Kentucky

Kentucky's farms and businesses grew after the Civil War. The state led the nation in growing tobacco. Many Kentucky horse farmers started raising thoroughbreds.

U.S. factories and railroads needed coal and oil. Coal mines opened in eastern and western Kentucky. Companies also drilled for oil. Many Kentuckians went to work in the mines and oil fields. People moved to the state to find work.

World Wars and the Great Depression

In 1917, the United States entered World War I (1914–1918). U.S. Army troops trained at Fort Knox, Kentucky. Kentucky's coal mines and oil fields produced fuel for the military.

The demand for coal decreased during the 1920s. Many of Kentucky's miners lost their jobs. Then many people in the nation faced financial problems during the Great Depression (1929–1939). Many Kentuckians lost their jobs, land, or farms.

In 1933, the U.S. government started the Tennessee Valley Authority (TVA) program. Many Kentuckians took jobs with the TVA. They built dams on the Tennessee and Cumberland Rivers.

In 1941, the United States entered World War II (1939–1945). Kentucky's farmers grew crops to feed U.S. soldiers. Kentucky's miners mined coal to fuel weapons factories. Other Kentuckians found jobs with the U.S. military.

Recent Improvements

In 1966, Kentucky passed the Kentucky Civil Rights Act. This law requires that all people

During the 1930s, many Kentuckians took jobs building dams in the state.

receive equal chances for employment and housing. Kentucky was the first southern state to pass a civil rights law.

In 1978, Congress passed a law to improve Kentucky's environment. The law says Kentucky mine owners must repair the land they mine.

Kentuckians also have worked to improve their schools. In 1990, the Kentucky government passed the Kentucky Education Reform Act (KERA). Today, KERA provides money to train teachers and buy school equipment.

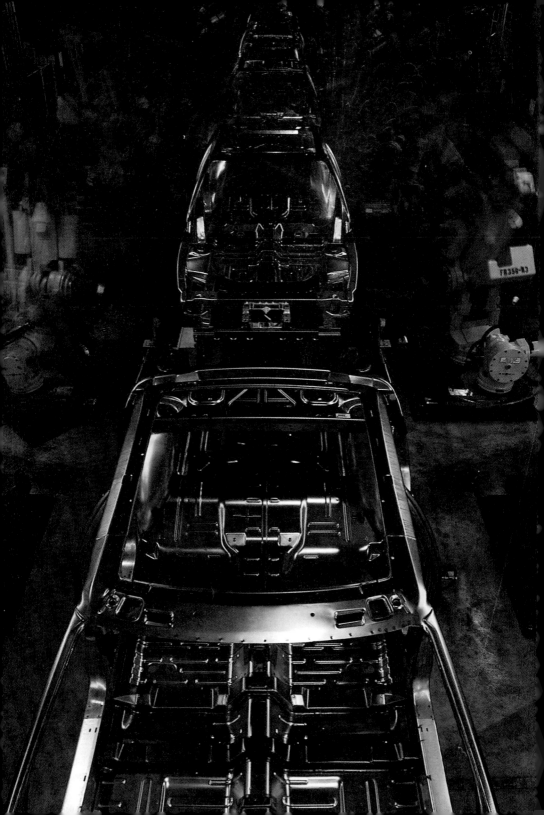

Chapter 5

Kentucky Business

Manufacturing is Kentucky's most valuable business. But most Kentuckians work in service businesses. Service businesses include trade, tourism, and government. Farming and mining are other important Kentucky businesses.

Manufacturing

Cars and trucks are Kentucky's leading manufactured products. Chevrolet manufactures Corvette sports cars in Bowling Green. A factory in Georgetown makes Toyota cars and trucks. Ford manufactures trucks in Louisville.

Kentucky's chemical factories make soaps, medicines, and paints. Other Kentucky factories make elevators and computer printers.

Cars and trucks are Kentucky's leading manufactured products.

Service Businesses

Trade is a leading Kentucky service business. People who work in the trade business buy and sell goods. Cars, trucks, coal, and tobacco are important Kentucky trade goods.

Tourism is another important service business. Tourists spend about $4 billion each year in Kentucky. Hotels, state parks, and shops earn much of this money.

The U.S. government and the Kentucky government hire many service workers. These Kentuckians work at Fort Campbell and Fort Knox military bases. Some service workers operate dams for the Tennessee Valley Authority (TVA).

Farming

Beef cattle and thoroughbreds are Kentucky's leading farm products. Farmers raise most of Kentucky's cattle and thoroughbreds in the Bluegrass region.

Tobacco is Kentucky's most valuable farm crop. Kentucky leads the nation in growing burley tobacco. Corn, popcorn, soybeans, and wheat are other important crops.

Coal is Kentucky's most valuable mining product.

Mining

Coal is Kentucky's most valuable mining product. Kentucky is one of the nation's leading coal-producing states. Coal deposits lie under 40 percent of Kentucky's land.

Oil, natural gas, and limestone are other important mining products. Oil and natural gas deposits often lie near coal deposits. Limestone deposits lie in many parts of the state.

Chapter 6
Seeing the Sights

Kentucky has other attractions besides
the Kentucky Derby. Many visitors enjoy
Kentucky's mountains, forests, rivers, and
lakes. Some take tours of the state's museums,
factories, and horse farms. Other visitors
attend craft fairs and music events
throughout the state.

Eastern Kentucky
Cumberland Gap National Historic Park is in
southeastern Kentucky. Visitors enter the park
on U.S. Highway 25. This highway follows the
route of Daniel Boone's Wilderness Trail.

Many visitors enjoy Kentucky's forests.

Daniel Boone National Forest is northwest of Cumberland Park. Cumberland Falls is in this forest. Cumberland Falls is the second-largest waterfall east of the Rocky Mountains.

Big Cities of the Bluegrass Region

Lexington is in north-central Kentucky. It is the home of the University of Kentucky. The university's Kentucky Wildcats men's basketball team has won many national championships.

Kentucky Horse Park is just north of Lexington. Visitors learn about horses there. Each June, the park holds a festival featuring bluegrass music. This style of country music features banjos, guitars, and fiddles.

Frankfort is west of Lexington. This city is Kentucky's capitol Workers completed the state capitol building in 1910. Visitors tour the capitol building and grounds.

Louisville is west of Frankfort. Many visitors take boat rides on the Ohio River there. The *Belle of Louisville* is one of the nation's last stern-wheelers. This type of steamboat has a paddle wheel in the back.

Other Bluegrass Region Highlights

Fort Knox is south of Louisville. The U.S. Gold Depository is there. The U.S. Gold Depository holds most of the United States' gold.

Bardstown is east of Fort Knox. My Old Kentucky Home State Park is nearby. A historical house there inspired Stephen Foster to write the state song "My Old Kentucky Home." Kentucky's legislature named the park after this song.

Visitors to Mammoth Cave can tour more than four miles (6.4 kilometers) of the cave.

Abraham Lincoln Birthplace National Historic Site is south of Elizabethtown near Hodgenville. Visitors to the site can see a cabin like the one in which Lincoln was born.

South-Central Kentucky

South-central Kentucky is cave country. Mammoth Cave National Park is there. It is one of the few national parks inside a cave. Visitors can tour up to four miles (6.4 kilometers) of the cave. Other famous caves are nearby. They include Crystal Onyx Cave and Horse Cave.

Bowling Green is southwest of Mammoth Cave National Park. Many visitors tour Chevrolet's Corvette factory there. Visitors watch workers assemble Corvette sports cars.

Lake Cumberland is east of Bowling Green. This is one of the world's largest lakes formed by a dam. Visitors enjoy boating, fishing, and camping at Lake Cumberland.

Western Kentucky

Owensboro is in western Kentucky. Owensboro is the Barbecue Capital of the World. Each May, Owensboro hosts the International Bar-B-Q Festival. Each year, visitors to the festival eat more than 20 tons (18 metric tons) of barbecued meat.

Land Between the Lakes Recreation Area is southwest of Owensboro. Kentucky Lake and Lake Barkley border two sides of the area. Visitors enjoy swimming, boating, fishing, and camping there.

Kentucky Time Line

About 10,000 B.C.—People are living in the area that is now Kentucky.

About A.D. 900 to A.D. 1000—Mississippian people build burial mounds in the area that is now Kentucky.

A.D. 1750—Thomas Walker enters present-day Kentucky through the Cumberland Gap.

1774—English settlers found Harrodsburg; it is Kentucky's first lasting European settlement.

1775—Daniel Boone helps build the Wilderness Trail; Boone and 30 other settlers establish Fort Boonesboro; the Revolutionary War begins.

1783—The Revolutionary War ends.

1792—Kentucky becomes the 15th state.

1793—Frankfort becomes the state capital.

1809—Abraham Lincoln is born near Hodgenville.

1818—Kentucky gains its southwestern tip in the Jackson Purchase.

1860—Abraham Lincoln is elected the 16th president of the United States.

1861—The Civil War starts; Kentucky remains part of the United States.

1865—The Civil War ends.

1875—Churchill Downs hosts the first Kentucky Derby.

1933—The Tennessee Valley Authority begins building dams in Kentucky.

1936—Workers complete the U.S. Gold Depository at Fort Knox.

1941—Congress establishes Mammoth Cave National Park at Mammoth Cave.

1966—Kentucky becomes the first southern state to pass a civil rights law.

1978—Federal law requires mine owners to restore mined areas to their original condition.

1983—Martha Layne Collins becomes Kentucky's first female governor.

1990—Kentucky's legislature passes the Kentucky Education Reform Act.

1996 and 1998— The University of Kentucky Wildcats win the NCAA men's basketball championship.

Famous Kentuckians

Muhammad Ali (1941–) Boxer who held the world heavyweight title three times (1964–1967, 1974–1978, 1978–1979); born in Louisville.

Sophonisba Preston Breckinridge (1866–1948) Kentucky's first female lawyer (1892); born in Lexington.

George Clooney (1961–) Actor who stars in television's *ER*; played Batman in the movie *Batman & Robin*; born in Lexington.

Jefferson Davis (1808–1889) Politician who served as president of the Confederate States of America (1861–1865); born in Todd County.

Duncan Hines (1880–1959) Cook and cookbook writer who founded the Duncan Hines bake mix company; born in Bowling Green.

Abraham Lincoln (1809–1865) Politician who served as the 16th president of the United States; born in Hardin County.

Loretta Lynn (1935–) Country singer and songwriter who is best known for her song "Coal Miner's Daughter"; born near Paintsville.

Garrett Morgan (1877–1963) African American inventor who invented the traffic signal; born in Paris, Kentucky.

Colonel Harland Sanders (1890–1980) Restaurant owner who founded Kentucky Fried Chicken (1956); lived in Corbin.

Diane Sawyer (1945–) TV journalist who became the first female reporter on *60 Minutes*; born in Glasgow, Kentucky.

Robert Penn Warren (1905–1989) Novelist and poet who won three Pulitzer Prizes (1947, 1958, 1979); born in Guthrie.

Whitney Young, Jr. (1921–1971) Civil rights leader who worked for better education for African Americans; born in Lincoln Ridge.

Words to Know

bluegrass (BLOO-grass)—a kind of grass that sometimes appears blue in sunlight

derby (DUR-bee)—a horse race

gap (GAP)—a narrow opening between mountains; Daniel Boone's group traveled through the Cumberland Gap.

jockey (JO-kee)—a person who rides horses in races

pennyroyal (PEN-ee-ryel)—a plant with purple or blue flowers

plantation (plan-TAY-shuhn)—a large farm where a main crop such as cotton is grown

sea level (SEE LE-vuhl)—the average surface level of the world's oceans

stern-wheeler (STURN-wee-luhr)—a steamboat with a paddle wheel in the back

thoroughbred (THUH-roh-bred)—a breed of horse born and raised for racing

To Learn More

Brown, Dottie. *Kentucky*. Hello U.S.A. Minneapolis: Lerner Publications, 1992.

Fradin, Dennis Brindell. *Kentucky*. From Sea to Shining Sea. Chicago: Children's Press, 1993.

Green, Carol. *Daniel Boone: Man of the Forests*. Chicago: Children's Press, 1990.

Harris, Jack C. *The Kentucky Derby*. Mankato, Minn.: Creative Education, 1990.

Lund, Bill. *The Cherokee Indians*. Native Peoples. Mankato, Minn.: Bridgestone Books, 1997.

Rodgers, Mary Augusta. *Country Roads of Kentucky*. Castine, Maine: Country Roads Press, 1993.

Internet Sites

Churchill Downs—Virtual Churchill
http://www.churchilldowns.com/kyderby.html

Excite Travel: Kentucky, United States
http://city.net/countries/united_states/kentucky

Kentucky Department of Education
http://www.kde.state.ky.us

Kentucky Historical Society
http://www.state.ky.us/agencies/khs/index.html

Mammoth Cave National Park
http://www.nps.gov/maca/macahome.htm

Welcome to Kentucky
http://www.travel.org/kentucky.html

Useful Addresses

Abraham Lincoln Birthplace
2995 Lincoln Farm Road
Hodgenville, KY 42748

Churchill Downs/Kentucky Derby Museum
700 Central Avenue
Louisville, KY 40208

Kentucky Tourism, Visitors and Convention Bureau
400 South First Street
Louisville, KY 40202

Land Between the Lakes
100 Van Morgan Drive
Golden Pond, KY 42211

Index